MW01602781

CHASM

The Hurting and The Healing

poetry by Dom Jones

edited by Meilani Clay

Sam,

Thank you so much
for supporting my work.
Hope you enjoy.

Dom

self-published by Dom Jones
For Dom Empire
©2021 Dominique Jones, All Rights Reserved.
Cover illustration and design by CreativePowerr

Printed in the United States of America.

visit www.iamdomjones.com for more information

First Printing: March 2021

For Octavia, Zora, Maya, Toni, Nikki, Alice, Nina, and Charlene. I hope I made you proud.

Paradox

they will say you never loved me
paint a mural of your hatred down dirty city streets
smear your surname in gold
like you never intended it to become mine
they will build a shrine
to your disdain for me
say you came for me only after the sun rose
on the other side of the earth
they will say that we were nothing after I never gave birth
call us a pyrrhic victory
that in the end the only rings exchanged
were the ones around our necks
those were the knots we tied
to swing from the rafters of our unfulfilled potential
they will say we saw ourselves
in their advice columns and self-help books
that we collected more dust than the epochs
written in our name
confined to an era, forgotten the next day
they do not know that I was the one beast
that you could never tame
a wild animal hungry for the moon
surrounded by stars and becoming one
i was blinding to a boy who'd only crossed state lines
once or twice
decades stacking on your receding hairline
and expanding waist
you tried to grasp the glitz you swore you never wanted
slipped through your fingers quicker than sand
and never left the residue of sparkle
as if I was never there
yet they'll say you never loved me

that mine for you was unrequited
never seeing me relinquish my disquiet for silence
my love returned, but turned magician
seen, but disappeared in an instant
I was gone
the one to find protestations welted at my figure floating
farther in the distance
and nothing if not thorough
I would leave mangled photographs of us
down interstates
like thousand piece puzzles for countries to put together
they would pick up the pieces like you never could
string masking tape from state to state
looking for the full picture
write like they had it
put us in storybooks they called biographies
you would read them in tears
defeat heavy between the lines they never caught
while making you the hero
you never saved this damsel who escaped your distress
now your distress calls straight to voicemail
but they'll say you never loved me
draw a line of patriarchy so deep in my face
it will look like a shank by the would-be authors
let the phone records fall at my feet
the calls are only coming from one side now
step over them onto crimson carpet
rolled out in front of me
been years since I had the inclination to look back
yet the statues are in your honor
exalted by history books feeding your frail frame
at my precipice you are falling apart
shrouded in what could have been
I am the one who has become

I am the one
who doesn't care enough to tell them
you loved me

Fin

when a friendship is over
it's supposed to hurt
that hurt should eventually become a dull ache
at some point
you shouldn't feel any more discomfort
it's like surgery
hurts badly at first
less at some point
then not at all

when our friendship was over (the first time)
I talked about you all the time
like you had died and I couldn't stop visiting your grave
I talked about you like you were the Lazarus of my life
I just knew God would raise you from the dead
I knew it wasn't dead yet
held onto memories like decaying corpses
refused to bury them
poured lavender oil around them to stave off the stench
of distance, time, and the dirt my friends tried to
convince me to topple upon them
you were coming back
I was convinced

when you returned
it was to help me bury the secret that would break us
out of my body and deep into my subconscious
you told me to tell somebody
and knowing that I wouldn't
knowing me so well even though
we were older and thicker
you took the day off

and drove the several dozen miles
to be there
you didn't hold my hand
you didn't tell me it would be okay
you didn't even make me pancakes
like you know I love to watch you do
you just sat there smelling like sandalwood
wearing gray
living in the gray with me
trying to wrap me in gray
knowing that I saw too many things
particularly this thing that was breaking us
in black and white
you loved me as we were breaking
loved me hard
more than I should have asked you to
but you knew
in this instance
you were the only one who could

when you sat at my mother's dining room table
my salmon croquettes next to your pancakes
we were supposed to be celebrating
I was leaving to do a thing that neither of us
dared believe I was brave enough to do
it was a somber celebration
much like our love
a pyrrhic victory
an anticlimactic goodbye
I choked down the aching feeling that
we would never see each other again
washed it down with cranberry juice
we both wore black
looking back

it was an omen
sitting at our own wake, having a final meal
I savored the pulse of your wrist
twisting the pan over the fire
the way your food sat claustrophobic in your cheek
I tried to make you laugh
enough to commit the sound to memory
I don't remember if we touched

when I finally unblocked you on Facebook
you were all up in my digital memories
it made me wonder if the ache would ever subside
if I would just be functional
with the chronic pain of our end
swelling at random, but mostly a quiet whisper
some will say that we don't know each other anymore
that we are mere phases in a lifetime
blips on longer paths
but I know all four of your names
the curve of your hairline is like walking ¼ of Lake Merritt
but I still know your order at the Hoagie shop
but it's over
finally over
never to be resurrected
gone

Jelani Tribe

I guess I wanted too much from you
knight in shining armor just isn't in your blood
it would be if you could
just show up
consistency is the thing
and you were easily distracted by the girls reflected in
your armor
chasing fast money and calling it wealth building
even in all of this
I found you beautiful and hilarious
wanted to wrap myself in the strength of you
but I was stronger
felt you breaking under the sheer brute of my gaze
you told me I was too intense
I added the "for a woman" in my head
a traditionalist without the means to be traditional
I found this ridiculous
how could you ask me to play a role?
while you were penniless
couldn't get me across a toll booth
much less happily ever after
so I kept the lead in our dance
watched you play a game
you assumed I'd join out of desperation
a queen is never desperate
walked away after
you dangled the first damsel in my face
the radio silence didn't affect you
until you heard my voice again
air shifts when royalty speaks
you were frantic
confused as to how you'd gone so long

without this tone in your ear
hastily promised me forever as though it hadn't been that
since we last spoke
hilarious. ridiculous.
your beauty still not lost on me
my heart lost to you, though
even as I dreamt of your lips upon my cheek
I awakened unable to fathom
putting my fate in your inconsistent hands
they would drop me to an early death
blame my weight
but know in your heart you just couldn't carry my depth
knees weak under my gaze
so how could I ever give birth
to the tribe of our friendship?
I would never risk a weakened bloodline
for companionship

Grown Up and Apart

your arrival an intrusion I braced for
but should have looked forward to
there was always something off about us
well…you
the way you complained about being judged
by your black parts
but rejected your blackness
while embracing caricatures of blackness
you were maddening
and even though I knew that all we had
were all these years
I let you land in my space
adjusted an impossible schedule for 48 hours
as my feet and heart ached to go home
you went on as though
I were both filler space and soul mate
confusing me with your violent wave
I let you grab my arm in the loud dark
forcefully pull me toward you
felt rage well up in me at the audacity
held myself and told myself to get a hold of myself
stepped between two strangers
quietly begged them not to move
told myself that even if you couldn't hold your liquor
that was no reason to hold me hostage
in your obvious pain and confusion
I would not be your death by consumption
filling your time with some high school dream
that would never come true
you told me you believed in me
I just wish you'd forget about me
forget this fantasy where our paths are parallel

let me off this carousel
one malicious touch and I was gone from you
I am not your padded room
not your ruse
to escape your reality
I bruise
but my skin will never turn shades by any man's hand
you woke the next morning
sending text messages as if it had never happened
but I was already a star breaking soil
and you, an asteroid crushing air trying to touch earth
you could never touch earth
not in a million years

Change of Address

why should I rep you?
much less respect you
wet you
is what the visceral anger deems necessary
wade you in streams of thought
leave you unresolved
a tension, hanging
swinging on the edge of nothingness
nothing less
than solitary confinement from my mind
bent on intentional erasure
graze you
with silver bullets that bleed you slow
alone in an alley no one passes
street lights burn deep into wounds
break your chest open
so you know what it feels like to be that
open you
split your skin east to west
surgical
let your organs pour out on my paper
accompany this sermon of silence
pentatonic pent up rage
rage you
against machines that raised you
blow up your schemes
on blogs and tweets
make you headline newspapers
collect paper off the red tape
you swore you'd swaddle me in
and all that disrespect you had in for me
karmically returned to sender

Nihility

we're going nowhere fast
faster than nowhere has gone before
a vast and empty space
the outer limits of nothing
lightning speed
racing towards an abyss that never ends
you, me, and nothing else
nothing behind us
nothing before us
and if we're honest
nothing between us
we're going nowhere fast
putting miles on my body
hoping you'll slow down
but you love that hollow action
looking into vacant eyes
while you drive into barren land
my eyes are too full
drive you away
but you always return
to take me nowhere again
stare into me, hoping to see desolation
but all I've got for you is destination
a desperation to believe we're destined
even though I know we're non-existent
going nowhere faster the older we get
your zero zips into me quick
no need to ask me if I got there
i'll never get there with you
if there is anywhere
if there is nowhere
i'm already there

still going
always coming
multiple arrivals
at nowhere

A Tale of Two Cities

the one from the east swore I loved
the one from the west more
yet I pray in the direction the sun rises
the northern lights in his eyes flicked off
a deep opal there like his skin
I reach out and touch his ghost in my sleep
awaken exhausted from the anguish he stirs
in my slumber
I am shaken
I am stirred
drunk in the spirit
cradling idealized memories of him in my bosom
the one from the east swears
the one from the west was to blame
and I've stopped telling him to watch his mouth
his swear isn't profane
because before his silence screamed we were finished
he sat with me in the clinic
invisible tears drowning
the one from the west's storm brewing
we never had to ask
can you stand the rain?
for the west was the rain; the thunder
the lightning in my eyes burning me blind
my lover and my beloved touching two different oceans
and the lesson that my love was never omnipotent
the biggest morning after pill that I forgot to swallow
I sent the one from the east drowsy, empty messages
sleepy hollow
and naturally, he started leaving me on read
the west would always answer, should I call
but I know I'll never bring myself to fall

his ghost chokes me in my sleep
an unconscious S&M that ravashes my rest
I reach out for the east to save me
but the east has flown west
now they're facebook friends
the fuck?
try to sage these ghosts from my sleeping space
now I get lost trying to decipher which one speaks
I'm lying
their voices are so clear
the east is deep and sends me spinning into frenzy
the west is basic and sends me running towards the east
there's just too much noise
yet his silence is the most deafening
three dots dance like he's about to break the curse
but the text never comes
I pass out from the insurrection in my heart
awaken to the sight of the sun rising
kneel its direction
head game vicious, but instead I pray
pray the east returns to me
pray the east returns to me
pray the east returns to me
the one from the east is consumed with the thought that
my compass is still broken
pointing west
I swear it's only you now
it was always only ever you
don't leave me for being lost at sea
all I've ever wanted was to come home

Halu
(which means "sweet" in Arabic)

it's best that you only love me back in my imagination
a monument made erect in my mind
I envision you love me exactly the way he hurt me
hard and consistently
that I look up to you the way he looked down on me
that we shine upon one another so much that he is
eclipsed and never mentioned again in this love poem I
write you

how can I love you so much
only having known you from afar?
heard your voice a million times on record
not enough live and in person
I play back your questions, pretending that your stanzas
are one half of conversations
and so I answer
lie your pages upon me
like I know your hands never should
I will drown in the reality of loving you
I will drown and you will save me and you will wreck me
and I will be wrecked
but you will never let me call myself wretched

so I dream of you in steam rooms
a towel around your waist and neck but otherwise bare
in these dreams I am always surprised to find
that your flesh gives in to touch
firm but not stone
firm but not stone
I imagine that this is the way you see my heart

that you are the only one to have ever seen my heart
this way
that you wouldn't change the makeup of my heart
firm but not stone

when I wake up, I still love you
it is an unreasonable love because
I don't know enough to trust it
you could be a villain
masquerading as my pusher and I fiend
but I love you too much already to believe
that you are anything other than the love I always
thought that I deserved but never received
a love that would swallow me up but never spit me out
a love that would let me be great, let me be strong
let me be all that I am innately

I love you so much
that even though I've put your love so high on a pedestal
that I know you'd disappoint me if it ever came to be that
we were lovers
I wouldn't be mad
I would pour myself upon you and press
praying that the pressure of my palm would please you
firm but not stone

but I think it's best
that you only love me back in my imagination
because from the little I know and the lot that I feel
you are everything that I've ever known I deserved
and if you were mine
I might cease to exist

I might become the woman I've always deserved to be

No One Else

when someone you once loved becomes a trigger
how you figure
I cope with all this love mingling with this pain
with this shame
I'm so ashamed that I still love you
after everything you've said and done
a body bruised, abused and tossed aside
now you say you've found the one
but I was your one when there was no one else
how do I look myself in mirrors
knowing I am culpable in my own misery
I could have walked away
love should have brought me home to myself
but it brought me to backseats and back alleys
where what we made was less than love
but more than fucking
left me feeling like a duckling you would never
call a dove
now you say you've found the one
but I was your one when there was no one else
was your Aretha
added to your chain of fools
had the tools to upgrade you
yet was broken and disheveled at the end of this affair
and you're moving on
my heart hungry for the potential
of what we could have been
but it will starve
a lonely end, drowning in this flood
now you say you've found the one
but I was was your one when there was no one else
fed you fortune from pennies in my pockets

draped you in magical worlds created by the most
ethereal timbre I could muster
lifted you with a crescendo
even as the life was sucked out of me
I let you live and shine and never asked
for a turn at being the sun
now you say you've found the one
and I feel I've got nothing left
but I was your one when there was no one fucking else

Inside Joke

thought my solitude would be a solace
solemnly swore I was set
solo was my line in the sand
sinking sand
sanding the tears off my cheeks
frozen by Boston winters
snowflakes pouring from unsuspecting eyes
these tears the suspect
the culprit
there's no quelling them
welling on my eyelids
lid blown off the well
well overflowing with water
inconsolable
uncontrollable
in control
quickly
quick enough to be unnoticed
noticeable distance
distant from disses
yet still dismisses
friendship
these tears the suspect
they're suspect
put your hand away
don't hold it out for me
I held out for love
love held me hostage
and I was love's accomplice
yet I escaped it
in favor of becoming accomplished
what did I accomplish?

but solitude
and no solace

Attainable Ugly

damsel in distress
damsel in this dress
damsel flip her tresses
he transgresses
she elects forgiveness since she can't forget him
she will never get him
yet she
will never give herself to another
stays pure for him
yet he sullies her water, wading in many streams
wading in women who called her sis
as if getting him inside themselves
is the most unspoken sneak diss
damsel in distress
damsel in this mess
of her own making
she's grating they always say
lucky he'll pretend to love her
don't know he really does
the casual sex between them keeps him from kneeling
his knees buckle at her breaking ground on building
something separate
but he's too prideful to admit all that she is
he pokes out his chest
between poking her
and all the others
and says he can do better
he says what she should be saying
damsel in distress
it's dangerous, the temptation to stay
to see him as safe harbor
to harbor feelings for safety from loneliness

he pulls out too quick after she comes
as if to remind her that
he can take away her pleasure at any moment
he is gateway drug and pusher
but she says she has it under control
there is no intervention coming
since they stay siloed between sheets
staff paper and high thread count
count bars between busts
crescendo and then nut
it's too much
damsel in distress
it's inconvenient to disconnect
the connection is strong
the connection is wrong
connection prolonged by fear
he fears she will get clean
push him out of her sea
he fears she will turn superwoman
he sees her cape, if she doesn't
what if she does?
damoiseau in distress
his breathing quickens cause she left
what if she is gone?
never to return

Through the Looking Glass

better safe than sorry
was always sorry
never safe
lock the safe
keep me out
lock our lips
so you'll never have to
say you're sorry
unspoken apologies
aren't apologies at all
play reckless with you
wreck me
mirror shows wreckage
are we wrecked?
try rinsing the stench of danger
from my skin
smoke soils my hair
I can't get the smell out
breathe second hand smoke
when we're not together
it's a broken high
I need connection
you ask me to apologize
for needing
connection
I do
I tell you that I'm sorry
for my natural inclination
inclined to climb this never ending incline
there is never life in the flatlands with you
only more mountains
only more mounting

you mount me
with wild abandon
a crook foraging sacred land
pillage the poet
you break my fourth wall
I can no longer act
like this is not
reality

One

if i was your one
I would one up every gesture of love
once upon a time you
one of a kind you
daily one on one
bring this home to you in one piece
never one night only
if i was your one

if i was your one
it would be one for the books
one in a million
my one and only love
would never let you become
the one who got away
if i was your one

if i was your one
I would let you figure out
more than one way to skin this cat
one way or another
you wouldn't become
a one hit wonder
'cause i'm all for one
if i was your one

if i was your one
I would be your dreams
all rolled up in one
and you would tease me about
my one track mind
get behind me

and i'll show you i'm not a
one trick pony
if i was your one

if i was your one
when you had one of those days
I'd show you why you fell for me
in one fell swoop
and I'd take care of number one
if i was your one
because you would be mine

Blanche. Dorothy. Sophia. Rose.

it wasn't love at first sight
my love was blind
wasn't interested in the way to your heart
time was healing my wounds
and the sea?
could keep all the fish it had
but love is patient
you were kind
became my trusted friend
and protector
your love meant never having to say i'm sorry
for being near you
my heart started skipping beats
odd meter when i'm with you
my heart beats in swing
and even though you made my knees weak
you never let me fall for you
reminded me that I could stand on my own two
but that you'd be there if i needed
I wanted to become your golden girl
thank you for being a friend
your heart is true
you're a pal and a confidant
and i can see you now
you gave me space to see myself again
and i do see myself
with you

West Oakland Niggas

he think he deep
deep as the ocean
deep as the center of the earth
deeper than bay area black men usually think they are
he's one of them but worse
doesn't try to mask his misogyny by calling me queen
calls me nothing but asks to smash
dares me to deny
him the benefits normally reserved for a husband
or at least a boyfriend
tells me no one else will want me
that i'm lucky to have him
that i might as well lie down
let him go deep
because the world is gonna end anyway
dives then tries to hip me to quantitative easing
tells me the economy been crashed
says we're already under tyrannic rule
he think he deep
I watch him spout philosophies
feel him spout his ecstasy
into my agony
I moan and he think he deeper
smirks like he's so satisfied with himself
tries to teach me a new chord
he's wrong
he's just playing an inversion of a triad
third in the bass
he think he deep
but doesn't even have the stamina to go another round
days. weeks. months pass before i hear him ask again
when i finally have the courage to tell him no

he tells me he can just call someone else
I wonder if she think he deep
looks at him with adoration
instead of the way i look at him with pity now
he tells me my music is dope
thinks i still need his validation
need him to go deep
but what we're both still learning
is that he never even scratched the surface

Nikon Negligence

do you know ya boy is a fuckboy?
of course you do
do you know ya boy was my nightmare for that long?
maybe not
we tried to keep you out of it
sometimes i looked at you
wondering if you would stand up for me
if you ever found out
started to tell you a million times
but didn't want to put you in the middle
it wasn't altruism
I was just afraid that if i told you
and you were passive about it
I'd lose you too
do you know ya boy is atrocious?
you know he is
laugh when it's other women
dap him up
what if you knew
that he was wrecking one of your best friends?
would you see me the same?
would you look through your lens
tears clouding your sight
and finally shoot my pain
with understanding
empathy
would you call him on it?
probably not
so i never told you
don't think i ever will
but if you read this and understand
that you're who i'm speaking to

how can you ignore it then?
ya boy is a mess
he tried to destroy me
you good with that?
you'll say no way
but your silence on the matter thereafter
will say something
to the contrary

I Am Woman

the only group of women surrounding me
as i tried to get over him
were the ones pushing past me to get into the lobby
or asking if i had an extra pencil
at night
I would plunge into opaque silence
curl into the fetal position
silent cries sure not to disturb my roommates
there were no glasses of wine
no brunches
there was no group retail therapy
I blew every work study paycheck
on ways to cover my grief
every comment on any garment
was proof that I was perfectly shrouded
neatly hidden
beneath color palettes that matched each season
it was only ever winter for me
I tried to build a group
a group of women to surround me
but they all acted scared of my cold
or feigned warmness in trade
for access to my access
eventually
I decided I'd get over him
on my own
wrote more songs in a week
than my peers wrote in a year
and they were all good
every single song
so i worked harder
rose faster

now when they pushed past me
to get into the lobby
they said hello
begrudgingly
their obligatory salutations rolled off
in tandem with my love for him
they didn't know
I was a burn victim
shedding death like they shed
proficiency songs in practice rooms
climbing out of the grave
he dug for my heart
by becoming known
if never liked
they didn't know
that their snarky attitudes
had nothing on a man
who plunged his hate into me
at every chance he had
broke me down piece by piece
transcribed my tears
to belt them back to me
water welts on burning flesh
and no women surrounding me
no one to say
"girl, fuck him."
I stomped through the snow
stomped through the rain
stomped through the sun
and no one ever dared to ask
about the footprints on my soul
just why i wasn't skipping

BITCH, I'M HEALING

get out of my way
walked out of winter
clutching my future close
and even though
those women never came
I came back to myself
a woman
roaring

Courting Ghosts

when you try to move on
from someone who's off
and all that he wants
is you on him again
it's walking a haunt
despicable ghosts of past selves
chasing you through night terrors
you hear him saying
that you haven't changed
you struggle to keep your heart
in the upright and locked position
he wants to take off
drunk
and with known mechanical issues
you grounded him for many years
but found yourself buried
under his sea of filth
you try to move on
he's off his rocker
he haunt her
the you that you leave with him
he can have her
he tries to get you to buy in again
but you're giving up the ghost
for new life
in the hereafter of years after
he races to capture you
face pressed against the glass
you're tempted to
give him a taste of your own medicine
but you've already tried healing him
tried breathing fresh breath on halitosis

that fool is rotten
dearly beloved
you were always forgotten
until you showed a glimmer of shine
then he swore he'd begotten you
claimed you were fine
but you are not his
you are mine
we are leaving him
we have left him
he is left
all those times he said you were wrong
you were always right
keep running
moving forward
don't look back
move on
let him remain off
and when you get on
send your ghosts
to keep him company

Sore Loser

it's not enough to buy candles
to take bubble baths
to drink moscato
it's not enough to buy new clothes
new shoes
move to a new city
feel pretty
not enough to get that matte lipstick
in every imaginable color
custom clothes from the motherland
not enough to be photographed
written about
it's not enough to win
win awards
win scholarships
it's not enough to win their hearts
if you are still fixated
on winning his

it's not enough to flirt with strangers
to live vicariously through fantasies
to live them out for real
it's not enough to make new friends
to laugh a laugh that sounds different
to say your trauma aloud
for the first time
to your sisters
to your best friends
to yourself
it's not enough to say you've won
won the battle
won the war

won the day
won it all
it's not enough to win your heart back
if you are still fixated
on winning his

it's not enough to cross that stage
to have them say you've graduated
earned the right to call yourself learned
if you haven't learned the real lesson
that you were trying to learn
this whole time
it's not enough to stack victories
document them in tweets
instagram pictures
facebook posts
likes and clicks
if the triumph you were aiming to achieve
still hasn't clicked
into place
it isn't enough to win your space
win that grammy
win the right to give master classes
win the hearts of the masses
if you are still fixated
on winning his

are you?

Spain

"are you gully?"
we'd say to each other
in unison walking outdoor
high school halls
she probably still thinks
to this day
that she befriended me
hanging out alone
in the bathroom
one day at lunch
our freshman year
the truth is
she needed a henchman
or henchwoman
smart mouth with no
real temper to back it up
I saved her from many ass whoopings
hop off the school bus and ask her
"are you gully?"
but while she chose college
I chose the studio
so the silliness was few
far between
holiday trips home
a winter break would
break us
the summer after i met you
for the millionth time
in the short time i'd known you
and loved you
and fallen hopelessly
you had me in some shit

so we needed to get outta town
because I didn't have to ask
you weren't gully
so i called her
told her someone had da sickest vendetta
she laughed and started
rapping 50's debut with ease
when i didn't join her
asked me what was wrong
I asked
"are you gully?"
can we stay at your place this weekend?
gotta get outta town
"what kinda shit you in?!"
she knew that even though i was her goon
I was mostly a square
said she'd leave the key for us
so we hit the road
why did i drive cowardice around?
she called me from the road
her man didn't want us to stay there
for years I blamed her
blamed her man
held you close
even though all i wanted to do was ask her
"are you gully?"
we stayed in a cheap motel
I drove you home when you felt safe
honestly
the threat looming
would have never stepped
like you, he too
was not gully
but me and v?

we were
and after that call
I never heard her voice again
she was the first friend I lost
fuckin with you

Keller Exit

you were my best friend
scales with a touch of bull
that's why we rocked so tough
lost each other to
the wrong people
I thought it'd be forever
carried that weight
a boulder in my belly
couldn't shake it loose
you were the one who
I could tell anything
now we're missing out
on every milestone
we reach
time passes and we
can't seem to get back
but for the first time
in a long time
I have hope
that someday soon
I'll be home
and i'll see you walking
down Telegraph
in a hoodie
with a fresh cut
and a piece of food
crowding your cheek
I'll ask you if you
need a ride
and even though
you won't
you'll oblige

and what first brought
us together
will do it once more
I miss you
still feel you
still wish i'd
have rapped over
one of your beats
and even though
I'll deny it if
anyone asks
I still love you
always will
to me
we'll always be
just a couple
of grape sodas

Tattered Trust

you never liked him
but i loved him
so when i finally
made the gut-wrenching decision
to leave
and you knew
how much it was hurting me
your cheer
the excitement with which
you met the news
a knife twisting in
my self-inflicted wound
you poured salt
like the aunt
with jiggly arms
who makes the best cobbler
and potato salad
your laugh a bitter taste
I washed down with my tears
we all knew
it had to end
but you met the conclusion
with so much glee
facing your broken sister
with no empathy
how could i trust you
with a feeling again
with any important news
of any gravity
when instead of trying to
lift the weight
that came with

leaving him
you just said you
never liked him
and while that
is a fair assessment
I loved him
so why can't you just
shut your mouth
and pass me a tissue?

Take it to the Grave

mama, i wanna tell you
everything between me and him
but i'm afraid
to throw my heartache
on top of everything
you've already
gone through in life
mama, i wanna tell you
that i chased him 'cause
he reminded me of dad
the good and bad
and i thought
subconsciously
I could rewrite history
make your love story
have a better ending
through mine
mama, i wanna tell you
that i was stupid
wreckless
but i also want to protect you
from feeling
that you didn't do enough
for another one
of your girls
mama, i wanna tell you
that he was the worst
but i thought i could change him
I thought we could be power
in the end
all we were
was calamity

mama, i wanna tell you
the way he manhandled me
ran roughshod over my heart
mama, i wanna tell you
that before i left for school
I learned the hardest lesson
cold and alone
on your turf without you
I wanna tell you
but i know it'll only bring
you pain
and i can't find it in me
to do anything other
than make you proud
mama, if i tell you
I know you'll be ashamed
and i can't bring you
any shame
awards
scholarships
degrees
money
I can bring you that
I will bring you that
oh, ma
I wanna tell you everything
but i don't wanna
see you cry
so i'll hold it
I'll carry it
the way you carried me
teach me, mama
how to push out
this pain

Stranger Things

how did i become a woman
who preached self-love
and independence
to young women
yet struggled in your web
of self-destruction
and co-dependence
to get free?
I ask myself if i was
a hypocrite in those years
question how to
atone for my mistakes
how to be accountable
for my part in the mess
we made
did we ever
make love?
or did we just
make friction
and potential life
that never saw light
how do i undress
from this heavy cloak
of shame?
I delve deep into the
abyss of who we were
try to finish the puzzle
so i can see
the bigger picture
why did i love you
so long?
why didn't i listen

when your gaze
penetrated me with
lust and leisure
I was nothing to you
yet i still let you
plunge hard
with everything you had
into me
left me wanting
more of the bare minimum
why didn't i
ever think i
deserved exactly
what i told those babies
was their birthright?
why couldn't i imagine
the kind of man for me
that i prayed they'd find
will i ever uncover
who she was?
the me that i was
with you
looks so unfamiliar
we'd have never, ever
been friends

Quantum Dom

dear 25 year old dom
you're at a crossroads
you have a good job
makin money
starting to do the things
you've always wanted to do
but you're in love with a man
and I use the term "man"
loosely
cause he acts like a child
you're in love with someone
who is not
on your level
and let me tell you
that you will not upgrade him
he will not get better
he will drag you lower
than you ever thought
you could go
you will make mistakes
that you swore
you'd never make
you will feel pain
that you didn't
know you could feel
you will keep up
a facade
masterfully
to the outside world
but dom
you will survive this time
in your life

this pain that feels
as though it will never
subside
will fade into songs
like rain fades
into receding tides
you will use this time
as timber
for a fire that will
keep you wrapped
in its warmth
for years to come
you will eat
off this pain
Dom
you will love again
it won't come
for a long time
you won't even
want it to come
sooner
you will give yourself
space to heal
time to plan
room to grow
your nights
will look glamorous
to your instagram followers
but they will be
lonely
you will use them
to write your future
to write your past
to write the things

that will make
them write you
checks
soon your king
will come
and you will not forget
that you once loved
a jester
a pauper
you will stand beside
your king
aware that you
almost lost your crown
to a clown
king will show you
who he is
remind you
who you are
you will get through
this time in your life
forgive yourself
for the ways you
broke yourself
for the ways you
allowed yourself
to be broken
give yourself
every chance
to become
me

love,

YOU.

Sum of our Parts

the edges of midnight in your skin
dawn in your eyes
I see a new day
everytime i look at you
a horizon across your shoulders
the future in the rise
and fall of your chest
I imagine walking into
this portal, a hand
tightly clasping yours
darkness as light
as the way my heart feels
when i'm next to you
next to you
I can be
anyone
but most importantly
myself
the wild child within
dancing in the middle
of your night
glide across
the ballroom floor
of your care
with abandon
fall back into
a life built
between our hands
held safely
in the infinite span
of a day that never ends
equal say

in where we're going
I will go with you anywhere
you will go with me anywhere
the safety of you
is exhilarating
I will take any adventure
you set before me
as long as your midnight
is beside me
to greet the next part
of an eternal day
in arms that never
let me go

But A Dream

you're hairy
this is what i think about
before i fall asleep
if we fell in love
could i put up with
the hair on your chest?
you eat an inordinate
amount of meat
would you eat vegan meals
sometimes
to make me happy?
the truth is
a you
and a me
in this context
feels like a fairytale
a dream that will linger
until the crust from my eyes
is washed away under
the heat and steam
of the shower
in fact
I never wake up
thinking of you
you only appear
in my mind
before i drift off
at day's end
so perhaps
we are not
meant to be
perhaps

you are simply
a lullaby

Personal Training

push me to the edge of my love
past the brink of comfort
i'm comfortable living alone
there is solace in having no proximity
to heartbreak
my heart is a couch potato
put me in conditioning
high intensity training
make this vessel do squats
kettle bells
build my muscle mass
push me to the edge of my love
make me stand in the ring with you
and play again
this contact sport
where we become a verb, a noun
more than an adjective
take me out of my imagination
into the eleventh round
at the eleventh hour
make me decide
to be pushed to the edge of my love
at the precipice
ask me to jump
to take a flight with you
that will never end
can you promise that it won't end?
you can't
keep my heart from racing
back to the couch
in front of the television
consuming fictional love instead of

consumed by real love
push me to the edge
on the fringe of familiarity
on the verge of devotion
push me hard enough
to fall

Mirrors

did i manifest the minotaur beside me?
feel the push and pull
it's a muscle ache between us
he wrestles his way
into my personal space
tells me
to let my guard down
I tell him
not to tell me
what to do
we lock eyes
like we'll lock horns
more like wrestling
than battle
and he holds me close
squeezes
like he's trying to wring out
all the pain i've ever had
rocks me in his grasp
plays my favorite song
the one i haven't heard yet
how does he know
just the right playlist
to unlock my door?
the bass soars
over the speakers
I'm still within his grasp
he won't let go
he promises
without ever saying
he won't let go
I'm greying

in his arms
I'm growing
my ears are burning
as he tells me everything
about myself
to my face
he knows me
knows my triggers
but will never pull them
dares anyone else to
stares them down with fury
the way he stares me down
with care
when i try to
run
he switches songs
asks me if it's really that
I want to go
or that i'm afraid one day
he will
he promises
without ever saying
he won't let go
squeezes me tighter
a plead in his embrace
asking me to
let go of
the past
and hold on for
this dear life
he wants to build
by my side
this minotaur
making every single wall

tumble
and taking their place
as my haven
I surrender

Deadly Sin

is liking you just a distraction
keeping me from seeing an unclosed wound?
will the wound ever close?
should i like you with an open wound?
the morning after the night you pissed me off
for the first time
i questioned if maybe i should just hang it up
perhaps i'm too particular to be loved
and since i haven't shared the particulars
of the last one i loved
you don't know what sets me off
so when i almost set it off
you didn't know what clicked
that particular button on
but maybe liking you is just a distraction
perhaps there isn't enough there
for me to open up my body
to more wounds
they think i'm hard
callous
but the truth is
I'm hard
when i love
there is no middle ground
I love you with every bit
or i don't love you with any bit
how do i know
if you're just a distraction
from the last time i split my heart open?
doctors sewed me up real good
but the scar tissue
is agonizing

could you love a wounded soldier?
hit on the front lines
I hear the better part of me saying
perhaps i should give you another chance
to piss me off
but i'm not even sure
if you even want it

Knock Again

i love you
hesitantly
you can't fully
tell the difference
but i can
take cautious steps
let you open one door
to find another before you
i want to love you
freely
but heartbreak has
taught me
that wild abandon
isn't beauty
that wrecklessness
finds me and love
entangled in wreckages
so i love you
with trepidation
you say i go hot to cold
the truth is i'm just
consistently tepid
feel the fire for you
burn inside me
afraid if i show you
the spark in my eyes
you'll burn me
with my own passion
you hold me
I hold back
you tell me
I hold the cards

I wonder if
that's true
awaken each morning
with a solemn swear
to open the flood gates
let my feelings for you
cover you
I imagine the bliss
on your face
as soon as you see me
let go
and i want to see it
'cause i love you
it rages through my veins
always at high tide
but the levee of my experience
keeps it at bay
I left the bay
to learn to love again
healed yet here
harken not to rush
feel the rush of surrender
pulse just beneath
the surface of my skin
when you touch me
you dare it
to break forth
herald the day
when my embrace
matches yours
I love you
without question
I know you feel me
hesitant

give me time
I swear to you
when you open
the next door
you will see
heaven
feel paradise between
the molecules of
my exhale
I've been waiting to
exhale
running from hurt
with held breath
you caught me
bated breath
baited breath
my lungs
rise and fall
to the beat beneath
your chest
I love you
just wait
just wait for me
I'm close by
I'm returning to
myself
let me give me
back to myself
and then i'm
all yours
for all time

Chasm

somewhere
there is a black girl
breaking
wondering
how she will
put herself
back together
proverbial
fetal position
she is curled
into herself
having loved
what she thought
was a mirror of
her black beauty
black girl
don't rush
to get up
you deserve time
to cry
to scream
to wonder why
to dissect why
to learn
to close that
gaping wound
don't let anyone
rush you to
your feet
there are no
ovations for
twirling through

the world
broken
feigning
functionality
fuck that
take
your
time
forgiving him will hurt
forgiving you will hurt
more
don't let a world
racing towards end
rush you towards
the end of your
grief
grieve
lie in the dark
rediscover your
light
somewhere
there is a black girl
wondering how
she will ever cross
the chasm of their love
questioning if there's
an other side
there is
I am there
waiting
to hold you

Acknowledgements

To my mama, for teaching me how to be strong.
To my sisters, for trying to be my mama, lol.

To Meilani, for consistency, sisterhood, being one of the
most resilient women & mamas I know.

To Jarrell, thank you.

To Oliver, for coming back when I needed you, if briefly.

To black girls and women who refuse to be broken,
who endure the most and excel the most,
who beat the odds, who change the narrative,
who are warriors, superheroes, shapeshifters, queens,
icons,

who hold space for each other, who hold space for me.

To Katia, a black woman, for the beautiful art.

Dom Jones is an award-winning writer, musician,
and creative entrepreneur from Oakland, CA.
She self-published her first book of poetry,
Boss Patois, in 2013. It was the runner up
in the 2014 SF Book Festival.

Dom graduated from Berklee College of Music in 2019,
and moved to Los Angeles
to pursue music and art full time.
This is her second book.

www.iamdomjones.com